TRUTH
ENOMICS

TRUTH
ENOMICS

THE SCIENCE OF ALLOWING ABUNDANCE THROUGH HONESTY

GERARD ARMOND POWELL

Health Communications, Inc.
Boca Raton, Florida

www.hcibooks.com

Library of Congress Cataloging-in-Publication Data
is available through the Library of Congress

ISBN-13: 978-07573-2442-0 (Paperback)
ISBN-10: 07573-2442-8 (Paperback)
ISBN-13: 978-07573-2443-7 (ePub)
ISBN-10: 07573-2443-6 (ePub)

Publisher: Health Communications, Inc.
301 Crawford Blvd., Suite 200
Boca Raton, FL 33432-1653

Interior design and formatting by Larissa Hise Henoch

**I dedicate this book to my sons,
Gerard, Patrick, and Teigan.**

And a special dedication to all entrepreneurs who are currently struggling to bring their dream and vision into reality in a profitable and efficient manner. Nobody knows the hard work and dedication that's needed in an endeavor such as yours. Whatever you do, do not quit; the world needs what you are creating. God bless you and your journey. I commend you for having the guts to become an entrepreneur.

CONTENTS

INTRODUCTION

I've always believed that literature has the power to change your life. I was never a great student in school, but reading had a major effect on my early success in business—one of the books that influenced me most was *Psycho-Cybernetics* by Dr. Maxwell Maltz. Published in 1960 and still in print today, it is one of the best-selling books of all time in the personal development category.

A plastic surgeon by trade, Dr. Maltz found the inspiration for *Psycho-Cybernetics* while working with the clientele at his practice. People would come to him, unhappy in their lives, and they believed the cause of their unhappiness originated in some aspect of their appearance. They believed there was an external, material basis for how they felt inside and, if Dr. Maltz could change how they looked on the outside, it would make them happy on the inside.

In many cases, Dr. Maltz was able to produce the physical change that his patient would request. If someone wanted a smaller nose, Maltz could do that, and the nose problem was solved.

But often, the nose problem wasn't the real issue. In fact, patients were often even more miserable after their surgery. They had believed they felt unhappy due to the size of their nose, but now, even with a perfect nose, they were still not happy. Despite their physical transformation, there wasn't a corresponding emotional change. Their unhappiness remained, and now there was also disappointment.

Utilizing these observations, Maxwell Maltz developed the concepts of "self-image" and "self-talk."

Maltz saw that over time a person's image of themselves could exist independently from how they actually physically appear. Their self-image would translate into an endless loop of negative self-talk that they would believe and act upon in every moment of every day.

Consider the implications of this principle in terms of how people think about their lives. A good entry point would be looking at how most people think of money. Many people think, *If only I had more money, I'd be fulfilled. If I had ten thousand dollars in my pocket right now, I'd be peaceful, joyous, and happy.*

But this is exactly the opposite of the truth. If your life were full of peace, joy, and happiness—which, by the way, is exactly how it is meant to be—abundance in every form would be immediately available to you, including financial abundance.

That doesn't necessarily mean you would be a billionaire. It does mean that money would no longer be a source of stress in your life. You would find the prosperity that you authentically need, regardless of what exact amount of money that may turn out to be.

Yes, you will get what you want. Yes, you will get what you need. The real beauty of it is that you'll know, for your authentic self, that what you want and what you need are one and the same.

Reading *Psycho-Cybernetics* in my early twenties had a profound and powerful effect on me although I'm not sure I fully or correctly understood the deeper meaning until much later. My initial takeaway was to not let a negative self-image get in the way of creating what I wanted. The emotional or psychological message of the book wasn't something I focused on in the beginning. Instead, I saw how its explanation of self-image gave me a competitive advantage in the world.

This perspective enabled me to combine my belief that everything I wanted already existed in the realm of ideas with the notion that I couldn't allow a negative self-image or defeatist self-talk to interfere. This gave me a sense of confidence that I had the ability to transfer what I wanted from the realm of ideas into the realm of my everyday life.

At that point, I was only interested in creating shiny and expensive material items. Since I didn't understand entirely how wealth creation really worked, I was enticed by objects and behaviors that were not in my long-term interests.

I created things that would bring immediate pleasure and excitement, but they were never going to generate true sustainable happiness. On the contrary, they would bring unhappiness and disappointment.

My life went that way for a long time; that's why I want you to have a better understanding of this concept than I did. So that your understanding of money will bring you authentic happiness rather than just momentary excitement or pleasure. Although I was always able to make money, it took me a long time to understand the difference.

One of the most interesting things about financial well-being is how people are so confused about it. You might think it would be very simple. After all, doesn't everybody want more money? Don't we all want to be rich?

But underneath the desire for wealth, there can be unconscious conflict. For instance, most people say they would rather be "good" than financially successful. This conveys a sense that rich people are not good people, so how can we have a positive relationship with money if we think that money is fundamentally corrupt? If we believe that someone's fortune was earned without honest labor, this derogatory impression of wealth can become even more distinct.

If you've grown up with the idea that "money is dangerous" or even that "money is evil," that mentality most likely extends beyond money. To a greater or lesser degree, you may have been raised with the idea that life itself is dangerous. As a consequence, even if you're not trying to be fabulously wealthy, there will be tension and negativity around your relationship with money. Eventually, this negativity will bleed into other areas of your life as well.

Have you ever really explored your beliefs about money? Those beliefs didn't come to you by conscious choice. Instead, you may have been affected by your parents' relationship with money or by some traumatic event that had a powerful and permanent influence—not just on how you felt about money, but on how you felt about yourself.

Furthermore, your relationship with everything (including money) is an expression of traumatic events in your early life that need to be resolved. I can't overstate how important it is to achieve that resolution. It's the foundation of *Truthenomics*.

"Do what you love" is a cliche of personal development books. There's truth to it—like all cliches—but this advice is more complex than it seems. If you love to ride bicycles, does that mean you should go into the bicycle business? Maybe so, but it's not necessarily a good idea to turn a fun activity into a way to earn a living because the activity might stop being fun.

However, it's certainly a mistake to pursue an enterprise that you dislike for the sole purpose of generating income. That will burn you out sooner or later. But it's amazing to see how often people convince themselves that a certain profession is their only option. If you want to be a tax accountant, that's great. Go for it. But also ask yourself how you expect to feel after thirty years of accounting.

Steve Jobs was a classic example of someone who found a balance of motivation. He was not driven solely by financial gain, and certainly not at the start of his career. Of course, after dropping out of college, Jobs needed money, so he responded to an Atari ad: "Have fun and make money." While he wasn't passionate about getting rich, he was passionate—compulsively so—about the possibilities of blending technology with design. That desire, plus a partnership with tech wizard Steve Wozniak, led to the creation of one of the world's most profitable companies.

Sometimes it may seem that we live in a time when pessimism is equated with intelligence. Murphy's Law says that if something can go wrong, it will go wrong—and Murphy's Law is often right. Still, overcoming negativity is a key tenet of *Truthenomics*. Being successful financially—with the right understanding of what that means—is an important step in that direction.

I wouldn't write a book about wealth if I thought money was evil or that making money was a bad idea. On the contrary, knowing how to create financial wealth can be a vital step toward creating happiness of every kind.

We'll look at the relationship between money and genuine happiness, which is a connection that some serious scientific research has explored. Here are several key points.

First, every person has a natural "set point" for happiness that is genetically determined. Some—relatively few—have a happiness set point that is naturally very high, and they're happy all the time. A certain percentage of the population experiences the opposite, and they are chronically unhappy.

Most of us are somewhere in between; we can be slightly inclined toward happiness, which has advantages, or we can naturally be a bit unhappy. That, too, can be beneficial, perhaps as a motivator for change.

Milestones and life events seem to facilitate short-term deviation from this happiness set point. So, if you were to get your dream job—and it's your dream job, at least partly because of the money it brings—then for three to six months, you would experience an elevated state of happiness. But after the peak, you would return to your happiness set point within another three to six months.

About 10 percent of our happiness quotient is

related to our social status, age, work, house, and car—all variables that can change based on our actions or outside circumstances. That's just 10 percent of how we experience happiness. So, where's the rest of the pie?

Above and beyond that 10 percent, everything that makes us happy derives from the choices we've made regarding the things we care about, things that money can't buy.

This can mean friends, family, outdoor activities, and romantic relationships. It can mean some form of artistic calling, like painting or music. It doesn't matter whether you're good at it. What matters is that you feel called to it from within yourself.

Based on this information, it seems as though physical things that made us happy yesterday or today will not bring us happiness tomorrow or further into the future. But here's the good news: once you understand where real happiness comes from and you make choices based on that, all the time and energy you wasted on anything else is given back to you.

This doesn't mean that you literally go back in time. It does mean that, when you really find happiness, you won't regret the journey that came before. You may even be amused by it.

Real happiness doesn't exist in the presence of anything except itself. That's one of the most mysterious things about it.

After I sold my last company, I retired from working, and I also retired from amassing one thing after another that didn't make me happy.

But what would make me happy? I spent ten years in "the pursuit of happiness." Gradually, I saw how the same principles that I'd used to create material wealth could be used to create emotional or even spiritual experiences and connections—happiness, love, relationships, peace, forgiveness, and more love.

You may have seen It's a Wonderful Life, the

beloved Christmas movie from 1946. Jimmy Stewart plays a hardworking family man who, year after year, puts aside what he'd *like* to do in favor of what he *has* to do for his family and his employees. The movie has a happy ending—sort of—but it deals with a problem that many people face.

Truthenomics teaches that this problem is self-created and inevitably self-sabotaging. There is really no need to choose between your dreams and your responsibilities. In fact, dreams and responsibilities are really two points on the same spectrum. Choosing between them is a logical contradiction.

Your first responsibility is to yourself, and your hopes and dreams form the very definition of who you are. There's nothing selfish about that. It's just a fact that needs to be recognized.

Unfortunate things will happen if you fail to do that—if you think it's wrong or even sinful to acknowledge your true identity. Sooner or later, you're going to burn out on being a slave to your perceived obligations. You're going to get frustrated, you're going to get angry, and you may even become physically sick.

You may somehow blame yourself for this, or you may blame other people. In any case, it's going to be a very negative situation, and it all comes from a basic misunderstanding of how to live. Don't buy into the false choice between dreams and responsibilities. Rather, create the belief that it is your responsibility to realize your dreams.

A key factor in wealth creation is seeing that spiritual life is not contradicted by material success. It's important to realize that even the greatest spiritual teachers—including Buddha and Jesus Christ—did not teach renunciation of material achievement. The Eightfold Path of Buddhism emphasizes the importance of finding your correct occupation or livelihood.

In the Gospels of Mark, Luke, and John, Jesus speaks of a coin displaying the image of the Roman emperor and says, "Render unto Caesar what is Caesar's." The historical interpretation of this quote pertains to the legitimacy of paying taxes. In a broader sense, the passage implies that we can and should participate in financial activity. We just need to understand the boundaries of that activity in the context of life as a whole. ●

CHAPTER ONE

No Expectations

Early in life, my prospects were not bright. The place I came from, the things that happened to me and around me, the things I had done and not done— all were pointing in a negative direction. The realities of my life were not good, and I was getting the sense that they were only going to get worse.

But from a young age, I somehow clearly understood how to bring things from the realm of ideas and feelings into the realm of material reality. At that time, I would never have thought of this as a power of wealth creation, but that's what it was. I looked at intangible thoughts as potentially tangible realities. The thoughts had not yet been created in the physical world, but they certainly could be created in the physical world. Most important, I somehow knew that I could make that wealth creation take place.

So far, so good. But because of the environment I came from and my limited exposure to a wiser point of view, what I chose to create was not always beneficial to my well-being. Often, I didn't use the things I chose to create in my own best interests or the interests of the people around me.

The main thing I chose to create was very large amounts of money. I've been there, and I've done that, but I don't want to distract you with stories about all the expensive cars I owned. Instead of what I owned, I want to focus on what I learned and share that knowledge with you.

My personal life has had many twists and turns, but I've had a wonderful financial life. That doesn't mean there weren't setbacks. But I've learned a lot about money, and while I was learning about money, I learned a lot of hard lessons about life as well.

While still in my twenties, I became a millionaire—and by that, I mean, I had a million dollars to spend. In my thirties, I took a company public as founder, chairman, and CEO, and my net worth was about $140 million.

Also in my thirties, that company I founded went bankrupt in the dot-com crisis, and I went completely broke. Actually, I was more than broke. I was six million dollars in debt, mostly due to the taxes and fees that come with ownership of a publicly-traded company.

That was when I was thirty-seven years old. At thirty-eight, I started my next company. I sold that company only three years later for a total of $89 million.

There are truths about human nature that I didn't know when I was starting out, which took many years to discover. I have now been fortunate enough to learn those truths—even if I often had to be taught the hard way.

There are also principles of wealth building that I intuitively understood to some extent then and that I'm now able to communicate.

This book's title, *Truthenomics,* combines two elements. It's about personal truth and personal finance, as well as how (perhaps unexpectedly) those two concepts are intertwined.

I want to clarify that my goal in these pages is not to write an instruction manual for becoming hugely wealthy. *Think and Grow Rich* by Napoleon Hill is the dominant volume in that category. I certainly recommend that book, but I'm not writing a sequel to it. *Truthenomics* includes information about money, but it also has a wider focus.

Beyond money, *Truthenomics* is about true wealth

creation seen through the lens of your relationship with money. It's about learning how your power of wealth creation can make money a positive presence in your life.

It's about discovering who you really are and understanding how that discovery can make abundance available to you—financially and in every way— even if you've lived with a sense of deprivation for many years of your life.

The questions that follow may look like a test, but they're actually something different. These twenty questions (with some commentary on the first ten) are intended to get you thinking about yourself by examining your relationship with money. As you think about that relationship, I hope you'll begin to see how different versions of those same issues appear elsewhere in your life, or perhaps even everywhere in your life.

You may want to think of other questions regarding your close relationships, career, or health. As you answer those new questions, you'll see how their foundation exists in the same thoughts and feelings as questions about money.

There are no right or wrong answers here. The purpose is to provide some real-world financial context in preparation for deeper self-realization.

MONEY SELF-REFLECTION QUESTIONS

1. If a close friend were having money problems, I would immediately offer financial help.
Yes or no?

Mark Twain joked that friendship is a wonderful thing that can survive all sorts of difficulties, except being asked to lend money. If you were asked for financial help by a friend, what thoughts would go through your mind? Would the amount of money make a difference? Would you want a legal contract? Perhaps most significantly, would you ever offer financial help without being asked? What do your answers to these questions tell you about money's importance (or lack of importance) in your personal value system? If you've ever been in the position of lending money to a friend—or of borrowing money—how did that turn out, and what did you learn?

2. I quickly get angry if I feel I am not being treated fairly financially.

Yes or no?

Psychologists generally agree that anger is a secondary emotion. Anger is the outward expression of some deeper feeling that won't or can't be expressed directly—and the deeper the feeling, the more intense the anger is likely to be. The truth is, all of us put price tags on our time, our work, and even on ourselves as human beings. When the correct price is not being paid, we feel fundamentally devalued. What makes this situation especially difficult is the reality that we should be treated fairly regarding financial issues. From a practical standpoint, keeping your anger to yourself is a step in the right direction for resolving financial conflicts. But that's not always easy. Honestly, it's often extremely difficult.

3. I like to daydream about being wealthy. Yes or no?

There's nothing wrong with having some entertaining fantasies. In fact, those fantasies can be useful, provided they become blueprints for real-world action. When picturing your life as a wealthy person, try to be as clear and specific as possible. What would you create in life to achieve your ideal vision of wealth? For many people, the obvious answer would be private planes, mansions, and expensive cars. But if you think about it a little deeper, are those things that could really represent abundance in your life? Toys are just toys, so have fun with them, even if it's only in your imagination. But while you're busy imagining: also think about the limits of material success and maybe ask yourself, "Is that all there is?"

4. I often worry about being poor.

Yes or no?

It's interesting to realize that most people who fantasize about being wealthy also tend to worry a lot about being the polar opposite of wealthy. While daydreams of riches can have some potentially beneficial side effects, there's nothing to be gained from a fear-based preoccupation with financial catastrophe. In some pathological way, this can even become a self-fulfilling prophecy. When you find yourself worrying about "losing everything," consider what needs you're unconsciously trying to fulfill with those thoughts and simply erase them as soon as they appear. Just imagine a big red stop sign telling you to turn around and go the other way.

5. When I wake in the morning, my financial situation is one of the first things I think about.

Yes or no?

Surprisingly, this is true for lots of people, but why? Or rather, why not? Everywhere we look there's a preoccupation with the material attributes of our lives, and every one of those attributes has a price tag. Naturally, we instinctively buy into that reality as soon as we open our eyes, and we can easily stay in it for the rest of the day. It may take a little self-discipline but try to begin your day with more spiritual reflection. You don't have to do a formal med-itation—although that's not a bad idea—but see if you can adopt a wider perspective at the start of the day. You can do it if you try!

6. When I go to bed at night, my financial situation is one of the last things I think about.
Yes or no?

You may have heard it said that, in the final moments of life, no one thinks about how much money they have in the bank or whether their tax refund will arrive on time. In the same way, there's nothing to be gained by ending the day mentally checking your bank balance—yet many people do exactly that. There really isn't much you can do about your financial situation when you're going to sleep, so just let it go. What-ever money you have will still be there in the morning. Plus, if you win the lottery overnight, it will be a very pleasant surprise.

7. I believe most people are honest and truthful about money.
Yes or no?

Oddly, sometimes very wealthy people seem unusually worried about being cheated or financially exploited, even over minor transactions. Millionaires worry about whether they've overtipped the server in a restaurant or whether their hotel bill was properly calculated. Maybe they question the honesty of others because they subconsciously worry about not being trustworthy themselves. Nevertheless, most people really are honest about money. Until proven wrong, you can safely give people the benefit of the doubt. You may be wrong sometimes but worrying about getting cheated all the time is really cheating yourself out of valu-able mental energy.

8. When you have lots of money, I believe that you can do anything you want.
Yes or no?

The short answer to this question is no; you can't do anything you want. That said, you can do more of what you want when you have the money to pay for it. So, if you have very little money, you'll probably find it difficult to do things that you might enjoy. In terms of being able to "do whatever you want," a bigger issue than how much money you have is what you actually want to do—and that's something you can always control, regardless of your financial situation. The biggest mistake is wanting to live like a wealthy person when you're not actually wealthy. If you avoid that, you really can "do whatever you want" because what you'll want is what you can afford.

9. The main reason for earning money is to enjoy life.
Yes or no?

As this statement is written, I believe it's incorrect—because the ability to enjoy life doesn't depend on money. But money can help you enjoy life, so maybe the statement could be rewritten with that in mind. It's also worth noting that some of the world's wealthiest individuals have come to the conclusion that the ultimate purpose of having money is to help *other* people enjoy life. Bill Gates, for example, lives in a 60,000 square-foot mansion and still has well over $120 billion at his disposal. So, what is he supposed to do, buy another mansion? Instead, Gates and his former wife, Melinda, have become perhaps the world's greatest philanthropists, helping a great many people and probably improving life for themselves as well.

10. I believe the main reason for earning money is to have security.
Yes or no?

From a philosophical standpoint, there is no true security to be found in this world. Everything can go to hell in a handbasket at any moment. But, unless you're prepared to live like a hermit, it's not a good idea to build your life around this viewpoint, even if it's true. In the absence of a complete disaster, there are many ways that money can provide security now and a legacy for your loved ones in the future.

11. If I won ten thousand dollars, I would . . .

a) Throw a party for my friends.

b) Put it in the bank and phone my adviser.

c) Believe this was part of a divine plan.

    d) Buy something I need or pay off debt.

    e) Buy something I don't really need.

12. My philosophy on money is . . .

    a) It's hard to get, so be careful with it.

    b) Life is short, so money should be enjoyed.

    c) Money should be shared whenever possible.

    d) Money comes and goes without rhyme or reason.

    e) The universe provides the money I really need.

13. When I have some spare money, my first inclination is to . . .

    a) "Shop till I drop".

    b) Do something that is fun but inexpensive.

    c) Buy something useful.

    d) Buy something luxurious.

    e) Think about ways to share.

14. My biggest financial concern is . . .

    a) I don't have enough savings.

b) I can't afford the things I want.

c) I spend too freely and sometimes foolishly.

d) I make less money than people I know.

15.   When I spend money . . .

a) I make purchases mostly on impulse.

b) I make purchases after shopping around for the best price.

c) I only buy what I need.

d) I buy quality items that last, even if they cost more.

16. My view on retirement savings is . . .

a) I regularly save money for my retirement.

b) I have too many other pressing expenses.

c) I'm making wise investments.

d) I don't really think about retirement.

17. When it comes to managing money . . .

a) I'm hopelessly out of control.

b) I keep track of what I've got and how much I've spent.

    c) I don't keep track of my spending.

    d) I rely on advice from people I respect.

18. **What would you do if a friend told you about an exciting business venture or investment opportunity?**

    a) Participate, even if I had to borrow money.

    b) Participate only if I could safely afford it.

    c) Research all the possibilities on the Internet.

    d) Tell my friend to be cautious.

19. **If you were asked to describe the financial environment in which you grew up, what would you say?**

    a) It was a wealthy environment.

    b) It was financially stressful.

    c) I was not aware of money issues.

    d) The money situation was always changing.

20. **If you see a penny lying on the ground, what do you do?**

    a) Ignore it because pennies are worthless.

b) Pick it up because ignoring money is bad Karma.

c) Throw it in the trash because it's just litter.

d) Save it because it's a gift from the Universe. ●

CHAPTER TWO

The Universal System

Despite my financial successes, or maybe because of them, my life became pretty chaotic, and I became a really terrible person. Drugs and alcohol were just a couple of my addictions, and I even tried to commit suicide multiple times. Finally, after causing a tremendous amount of pain to myself and others, I checked into rehab.

That decision, described in my previous book, *Sh*t the Moon Said,* led me to experience plant medicine that finally freed me from a destructive cycle of addiction and suffering. It was a miracle, and I learned that it was a replicable miracle. At Rythmia Life Advancement Center, the plant medicine resort in Costa Rica, I've seen that miracle occur time and time again.

How did that miracle work for me? Plant medicine revealed the mechanisms of wealth creation that I had been exploiting but did not fully understand—it showed me how I was able to create so much money in my youth. It also showed me that everybody else who knows how to make money operates in the same way. Beyond the creation of wealth, this revelation further illustrated the essence of the universal system that I had tapped into financially but was missing in every other facet of my life.

the four CIRCLES

These four circles are a blueprint for achieving what you want in life—what you *really* want, not what you've been told to covet or taught to expect. When you understand the four circles, everything that seems mysterious will become perfectly understandable.

The four circles are like a bird's eye view of the process of wealth creation. That includes money, but it's not limited to money. When I refer to wealth creation in these pages, I mean the creation of positive abundance in any and all forms. By the way, a large amount of money is not necessarily a positive resource. Maybe it's just a large amount of money, or maybe it's a negative influence, but it's not automatically "wealth" in terms of *Truthenomics.*

Before we continue, you'll need to clearly grasp the meaning of each of the four circles, especially the first three circles. It will be critical to know who you were (and actually still are) at the level of your soul. It's also vital to know how you became separated from that soul identity and became the person you are in this very moment. Once you are crystal clear on those two realities, you can then understand what it is that you most authentically desire. Then, almost miraculously, the Universe helps you get to where you want to go.

To progress through the four circles, we can start by analyzing how they work together in an organized, systematic fashion.

In my own life, considering where I started and how messed up I was in the beginning, it's surprising that I genuinely accomplished my goal at the time—and that goal was just to make a ridiculous amount of money. It was difficult for my friends and family to understand how that happened, and it was also hard for me to understand.

This was something that I asked about in my early experiences with plant medicine: Why had I done so well despite my disadvantages?

The answer was very clear: I had become wealthy

because of my intuitive understanding that wealth building happened according to a system. I also had an inherent understanding of how the system of wealth creation works.

The laws of wealth creation are the same for wealth in every form—love, money, or whatever it is that you're looking for. It's the same system, the same law. It's as consistent and deliberate as the law of gravity.

If I drop a pen, it's going to do one thing for sure. It's going to land on the floor. If I drop it a hundred times, it's always going to do the same thing because of the physical law of gravity. It doesn't matter who's dropping the pen, what time of day it is, or whether the pen has red or black ink. When you drop a pen, it will always land on the floor. The laws of wealth creation are exactly that consistent.

Once you understand this, a whole new way of looking at wealth creation will appear. Many of us, maybe because of how we were brought up or because of our religious beliefs, think that there's a moral dimension to money. We may think, for example, that nice guys finish last; you can't be wealthy if you're a nice guy.

At the same time, we may believe that God, who is good, rewards people who are also good. So, is everybody wealthy somehow good, no matter how they may appear?

Neither of those viewpoints is on the right track because wealth has nothing to do with morality. Every day you can read about some terrible person who's making a fortune, and you can also read about very ethical rich people. Still, they both use the same system for success. The laws of wealth creation do not discriminate between people who are good and people who aren't.

Besides thinking that wealth is related to the vices or virtues of whoever manages to acquire it, many people believe that wealth is bad in itself. That notion even seems to appear in the teachings of

Christianity. After all, Jesus said that it is easier for a camel to pass through the eye of a needle than for a rich person to enter heaven. In other words, it's very difficult to be both rich and spiritually enlightened.

For some people, money does get in the way of spiritual truth. But can't poverty also be an obstacle to spiritual connection? It may be hard for a rich person to go through the metaphorical eye of a needle, but that doesn't mean it's any easier if you're poor. In fact, as someone who's been both wealthy and poor, I can assure you that spiritual progress is easier if you don't have to worry about paying for groceries. So, what is the secret to wealth creation? The first step is knowing who you are to begin with. ●

CHAPTER THREE

Who You Were, Who You Are

As you begin thinking about the laws of wealth building, you should realize that your life as a human being is already an incredibly successful example of the system of wealth creation. Essentially, you yourself are both an example of wealth creation and the system behind wealth creation.

Here's an example of what that means: right now, the population of the Earth is about seven billion people. For those seven billion births to take place, how many potential births did not take place? You've probably heard about the vast number of sperm that fail to fertilize an egg, right? Well, multiply that by seven billion.

But that's not all. Think of all the earlier chances of fertilization that did not take and how they set the stage for the current population to have their opportunity to be born. It's an unimaginably large number, but out of that immense number, out of those hundreds of thousands of zeros, you were created. You are here, and trillions of others are not.

Congratulations, you created yourself into this existence. You were a four hundred quadrillion-to-one long shot. Don't ever sell yourself short when it comes to wealth creation, and don't convince yourself it's out of reach. The lottery-winning wealth creation that has brought you to this page did so for a good reason. That reason is nothing less than repairing and restoring your connection with the wholeness of your soul.

However, that's not the end of the story. It's true that you've already accomplished some truly miraculous wealth creation(s), but everybody else on the planet has done the same thing. Yet very few people have created wealth, financially or otherwise. Truth be told, over the past several decades in the United States, there has been a widening gap between a small number of wealthy people and everyone else.

The laws of wealth are not especially complicated, and putting them to work for you is also not difficult to understand. Actually doing it, however, is not easy. If it were easy, a lot more people would be wealthy. You've got to make a serious commitment to creating wealth through the universal system. That's the first essential step.

The second step is to clear your mind of whatever ideas you've got about how to create wealth in your life—because unless you're wealthy already, those ideas have obviously been wrong.

Third, you've got to lose whatever guilt you feel about your desire to create wealth. Like all the laws of wealth building, that desire is morally neutral. Wanting to be wealthy doesn't make you good or bad, so erase that idea from your mind.

How can you accomplish these steps? You need to start from the beginning. Instead of starting with what you know now or what you think you know now, we're going to start with what you used to know but have long since forgotten.

At one time, you existed as just a tiny blip of energy. You were the smallest possible entity, what physicists call quanta. As you expanded from that state, when you were preparing to be born and getting ready to come into the world as a human being, there were a lot of things you didn't know yet, but there were two things you did know—and those two things are key elements in building wealth.

First, you knew who you were at that moment.

Second, you knew exactly what you wanted.
You knew you wanted a human body,
and you wanted to live a life.

Those two bits of knowledge were the basis for everything you initially created—your entrance into the world, your mother, your father, your identity as an individual human being, and all the rest of what you would experience in earth school.

To build wealth for the purpose of finding happiness, you will need to reclaim and connect with who you came here to be and your deepest desires for this experience. But first, you need to accurately recognize who you are in this moment. In other words, who is the person that you have become?

Who is the personality you've become compared to the person you are, always have been, and always will be in your deepest and most authentic self? ●

CHAPTER FOUR

Through the Looking Glass

Here's a simple experiment that you may find both surprising and revealing. You'll need two simple tools: a small mirror and a dry-erase marker to write on the mirror. That's all it takes.

Look into the mirror from about eighteen inches away, just far enough to see your full head and your face.

When you look in the mirror, what you see is a perfectly accurate representation of your physical self, right? There's no doubt about it—this is what you look like. Except it isn't.

For one thing, as you probably know, the image is reversed. Right is left, and left is right. Everything is backward, but that isn't the only interesting thing about the mirror image.

As you look in the mirror, take the dry-erase marker and trace the outline of your head and face. As you do this, you'll notice that the outlines you've drawn are smaller than the physical realities—not just somewhat smaller, but dramatically smaller. In fact, the image is only about the size of your closed fist.

When you looked in the mirror, you were confident it showed how others see you. But it's really only how your reflection in a mirror looks. Your authentic reality is something very different and much deeper than that reflection.

So, who are you really, beyond even your

best-educated guess in the present moment? Who are you beneath the deceptively convincing evidence in the mirror? And how did that evidence become so convincing that you completely bought into it?

In the first few years of the twentieth century, a couple of very important things happened. One of these developments changed how we think about the universe, and the other changed how we think about ourselves.

Albert Einstein showed that time and space were flexible, which had huge implications for science. Einstein introduced a new meaning of the word *relativity*. But as far as everyday life was concerned, the writings of Sigmund Freud, the inventor of psychoanalysis, had a more immediate impact. While Einstein redefined *relativity*, Freud redefined *trauma*.

Before Freud, painful and traumatic experiences in early childhood were viewed fatalistically; people would just try to forget about them or at least cover them up. They would, at most, repeat the stories of their childhood tragedies to people around them for years to come.

Freud's huge innovation was making an explicit connection between painful events in a person's early childhood and psychological problems later in life. As Freud's influence grew, the meaning of the word *trauma* radically changed.

Previously, *trauma* referred only to a physical injury, like a cut or a broken bone. A person with a severely broken leg might walk with a limp for many years afterward. These were the only type of post-traumatic effects that had been recognized, but Freud extended the definition of trauma to include emotional experiences.

According to psychoanalysis, seeing or hearing disturbing things could be just as traumatic as severe illnesses or serious injuries. The aftereffects could be just as damaging and long-lasting, even if the aftereffects were psychological rather than physical.

It took some time for this idea to really take hold in the general American population. Even through the Great Depression of the 1930s and World War II, few Americans would have been comfortable describing themselves as emotionally traumatized. To do so would have suggested weakness or even—if a psychiatrist got involved—"craziness."

But times have really changed. It's rare today to find anyone who does not feel that they were somehow hurt, scarred, or painfully misunderstood in their developmental years. By the time they're six or seven years old, virtually everyone has gone through some kind of traumatic experience. Some people are willing to talk about it, some people can't stop talking about it, and some people keep it to themselves.

But I want to reframe the whole meaning of early life trauma, and that process of reframing is the foundation of *Truthenomics.*

Truthenomics means that we should not ignore the trauma that caused the loss of our original wholeness, but we must not endlessly regret it either. Instead, we must grasp the power to regain our wholeness—to connect with who we were so that it becomes who we are right now.

REGAINING WHOLENESS

We need to do more than just recognize that something is missing and feel bad about that loss. We need to regain what was lost—and that takes mental and spiritual work. It won't happen by itself.

In your wholeness, in your original and authentic self, you are love, you are beauty, you are happiness, you are all those wonderful things. When you finally know this and reconnect with who you originally were, that experience will radically change who you are in the present moment.

But if you don't know who you are in your wholeness—essentially who you were naturally as a child, which most people don't know—the lack of that understanding will negatively influence who you are right now. What you want in this moment will not be what you want in your original and authentic identity. In fact, what you want when you're out of touch with your wholeness will always be an attempt to bridge that separation.

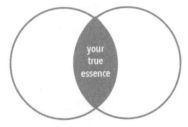

As you look at this diagram, think of yourself in your wholeness on the left and who you've become on the right. You are both of those entities. The goal is to merge into one (the center) and reclaim your soul, which contains your true essence and the purpose for your existence. ●

CHAPTER FIVE

To Get Where You Want to Go, Know Where You Are

To create true wealth, you must reconnect with your soul self, the authentic wholeness that you brought into the world. To establish that reconnection, you first must understand *exactly* who you are right now in this precise moment. To know the person you really are, beyond time and space, you must know exactly who you've become right here and right now.

Without forgetting or ignoring the traumatic experience that led to separation from your soul self, you need to reject any form of victim consciousness.

You need to accept the fact that through your actions, thoughts, and feelings, you have created everything that makes up your life right now. You need to own it. All of it.

You have to understand your strengths, your weaknesses, what you're good at, what you're not good at, what you like, and what you don't like. Most importantly, you have to understand what you want and why you want it. Simply put, you have to know *yourself*.

What happens if you don't know these things? What happens if you're in the dark about who you are right now?

Imagine you're in New York City at the Empire State Building, and you want to visit the Statue of

Liberty. You call a taxi company, and they ask where you need to be picked up.

But instead of giving your current location at the Empire State Building, you say you're at Yankee Stadium. Maybe you actually believe you're at Yankee Stadium. It doesn't really matter because one thing is for sure—the taxi isn't going to pick you up at the Empire State Building. You're not going anywhere until you know your current location and are able to communicate that information. Because the Universe can't find the person you're pretending to be.

Asking people for help with who you are right now can be very helpful. Of course, the people you ask will need to know you really well, and they must feel completely certain that you want to hear the truth as they see it. Don't give anyone the impression that you expect some sort of deep evaluation of your soul. You just want to know what you're really like at this moment, with the understanding that you've probably been different in the past and you will almost certainly change in the future.

As I've mentioned, I got into quite a bit of trouble when I was young. If there was anything good about that, it was the fact that it provided a very clear picture of exactly who I was.

I looked at myself, and I saw a kid who had just gotten out of jail and who didn't have a high school diploma. That was me.

Here's the beauty of that kind of realization.

The second you have a clear picture of who you are in the moment, the picture changes—because now you have awareness.

The Universe is constantly trying to tell us who we are, and we spend a huge amount of time and energy trying to evade those truthful messages. We are always trying to flip those messages into something else because we are so incredibly afraid of the truth.

If you deny the truth, nothing will change. The longer you deny the picture that's being shown to you, the longer that picture shows exactly the same thing. Who you are now remains frozen in time.

The moment you say yes to what the Universe is telling you, that's the moment when change happens. Because the Universe can't change who you're pretending to be.

Too many people waste large amounts of energy creating visions of themselves that are out of sync with who they really are now. That can involve a lot of excuse-making. People play a bad game of golf, and they make excuses to firm up the idea that they're excellent golfers. It must have been because the clubs were no good, right? But once you connect with who you really are now—even if you're someone who is really not good at golf—then the Universe will be in sync with you.

Suppose you say, "I want to be good at golf even though I'm not good now." When you adopt that perspective, it opens up a whole new range of possibilities.

The self-assessment questions that follow can help you more accurately define who you are at this moment in your life. This is an essential step in the process of discovering who you are in your deepest, truest self—and therefore responding thoughtfully to each question is an essential part of *Truthenomics.*

Many more questions about your present self may occur to you, and I urge you to consider as many of them as possible. You may want to write them down or just give them some thought. Either way, try not to think of the questions as only in the abstract. See if you can produce specific examples to support your responses.

There are no right or wrong responses, so there's no "grade" for these questions at the end. The purpose is to get you thinking, nothing more and nothing less.

In response to the questions, you can choose

from three levels of possibility: You may agree that the statement applies to you. Alternatively, you may feel that it doesn't apply, or, finally, you may feel the truth is somewhere in the middle, and the statement applies only sometimes or rarely. You can indicate your responses on a three-point scale:

"Not at all" means this never applies to you.

"Somewhat" means there are times when it does and times when it does not apply to you.

"Very" means it strongly applies to you.

SELF-ASSESSMENT QUESTIONS: WHO ARE YOU IN THIS MOMENT?

1. Do you consider yourself to be trustworthy?

Not at all   Somewhat   Very

2. Do you finish jobs/tasks you begin?

Not at all   Somewhat   Very

3. How happy are you?

Not at all   Somewhat   Very

4. Do you frequently find fault in others?

Not at all   Somewhat   Very

5. Are you a peaceful person?

Not at all   Somewhat   Very

6. Are you an outgoing person?

Not at all   Somewhat   Very

7. Do you get angry often?

Not at all   Somewhat   Very

8. Are you an energetic person?

Not at all   Somewhat   Very

9. Do you feel emotionally stable?

Not at all   Somewhat   Very

10. Are you lazy?

Not at all   Somewhat   Very

11. Do you forgive people easily?

Not at all   Somewhat   Very

12. Are you assertive?

Not at all   Somewhat   Very

13. Do you stay calm in tense situations?

Not at all   Somewhat   Very

14. Do you consider yourself to be intelligent?

Not at all   Somewhat   Very

15. Do you consider yourself to be successful?

Not at all   Somewhat   Very

16. Are you helpful to others?

Not at all   Somewhat   Very

17. Do you like to argue with people?

Not at all   Somewhat   Very

18. Are you organized?

Not at all   Somewhat   Very

19. Are you stubborn?

Not at all   Somewhat   Very

20. Are you selfish?

Not at all   Somewhat   Very

Now, in the spaces below, write five words that accurately describe who you are today:

1. _____

2. _____

3. _____

4. _____

5. _____

As you look over all your responses, are you surprised by any of your self-assessments? Are there any of your self-assessments that you believe other people would find surprising? What traits would you expect other people to find in you? ●

CHAPTER SIX

What You Want, and Why

We've seen the importance of reconnecting with who you are in your authentic wholeness, and we've also seen how that depends on a crystal-clear picture of the person you've now become.

When that clear picture has come into focus, you have gained the power to reconnect with your soul self, your authentic self, and to see the world from the perspective of your wholeness. That changes everything.

With the benefit of that beautiful knowledge and insight, you can ask some big questions that will allow you to find answers that were invisible to the person you've been while disconnected from your wholeness.

Now, what do you *really* want to bring into your life? What do you really want to get from your life? And why?

If you want more money, why do you want it?

What do you want to do with that money? What does it feel like? What does it look like?

If you want loving relationships, what can you do to bring those relationships into your life? Do you know anyone right now with whom you can create that kind of loving relationship? If not, what steps can you take to meet the kind of people with whom you can find fulfillment?

It's impossible to know what you want if you don't

know exactly who you are. Not just who you are in this moment, but who you've become from your earliest moments in the world. Once you know those things, knowing what you want becomes easier and easier.

When I got kicked out of school and started working without a high school diploma, I knew I wanted to have a million dollars. Not just "a lot of money," but "a million dollars." It was all very specific in my mind, not at all an abstract concept.

I knew what a million dollars would look like in twenties, hundreds, and even tens. I knew how a million dollars could fit into a briefcase. I knew how that money would feel and how it would smell. I even knew how it would taste.

That was where my consciousness was at during that time. It wasn't a very advanced state of consciousness, and if someone had asked me to describe it, I probably wouldn't have been very articulate. I wasn't truly aware of the person I was, and I couldn't get enough distance from that person to be insightful about him.

All that has changed for me now. I know that I want true wealth and what I need to do to achieve true wealth. I know it from the perspective of my wholeness.

What does true wealth mean to you from the perspective of your own wholeness? You have to know in such precise detail that you convince yourself that you already have it. Once you convince yourself that you already have wealth, actually obtaining wealth becomes extremely easier.

We can understand this as a mystical concept, but it's also been proven in down-to-earth ways. In a well-known research study, two groups of high school basketball players practiced shooting free throws. One group practiced with an actual ball and basket. The players in the other group only closed their eyes and imagined making perfect shots.

When the players were tested at the end of the

study, the "imaginary" shooters had improved just as much as the others. What happened in the players' minds had a positive influence on what they were able to do with their bodies.

Without knowing of the basketball experiment, I used a version of this in my own life. When I was in my early twenties and working as a bellman in a hotel, unloading people's suitcases, I could see myself in a mirror and think, *There's a millionaire. That's what a millionaire looks like.* I was living in a wealthy person's reality, even if I was the only one who knew it.

I projected that experience to everybody around me. My coworkers thought I was crazy, but I kept believing I was a millionaire with absolute determination and conviction. Then one day, somebody came through the door and noticed that characteristic about me and gave me a job that allowed me to make my first million dollars.

That was great, and it was exactly what I wanted at that time. But what was even greater was how—by knowing what I wanted and getting it—I learned that what I *really* wanted was something much different and much greater.

So many of us cheat ourselves out of what we want because we don't really understand what it is we want. We believe somebody else's story of what we're supposed to want instead of honestly exploring our authentic desires and needs.

What you want right now changes as you reconnect with your soul self, but remember that can't happen until you recognize the person you have become and take full ownership of everything in that person's life.

As we've discussed, most of us are still tied to the experience of a traumatic incident from early childhood, often around the age of five. This is a kind of enslavement by the past, and *Truthenomics* can break you free. There's no justification for living with that kind of slavery today or believing that you have to be a shoemaker because your father was a shoemaker.

The clearer you are about the person you have become, the sooner you reconnect with the person you truly are and were meant to be. ●

CHAPTER SEVEN

The Vehicle Will Appear

The ancient civilizations of Mexico and Central America had some fantastic accomplishments: huge pyramids, great cities, magnificent sculptures, sophisticated astronomical charts, and much more. But there's one thing that sets those cultures apart from ancient civilizations in other parts of the world and perhaps prevented the Aztecs and the Mayans from being even more accomplished than they were.

The ancient people of Mexico and Central America never made use of humanity's single most important mechanical innovation. They never used the wheel in their monumental projects.

Please note that I've tried to phrase this observation very carefully. I haven't said that the Aztecs never invented the wheel or never discovered it. I've said that they never used it to create their best-known accomplishments. But they did know about the wheel, and they used it—not to build their cities— but for their children's toys. They were aware of the wheel and how it worked, but they didn't see all its useful applications.

Some important principles of *Truthenomics* are at work here. First, the fact that you don't "see" something doesn't mean that it isn't there. Second, you may see something, but you don't recognize how you can put it to use.

Maybe you see it and understand what it can do,

but you don't have any real use for it, at least not at the moment.

Probably all these factors were at work when civilizations failed to make use of a revolutionary innovation like the wheel—and their mistakes seem obvious when we view them from a distance of centuries. But our own blind spots are indeed our blind spots. Sometimes, our blind spots keep us from being the best version of ourselves or block us from the opportunity to grow in order to survive. Recognizing our blind spots and opening our eyes to opportunity takes effort and imagination. But all that is amazingly worthwhile.

Let's assume you've come to recognize an activity that genuinely makes you happy. Suppose it's hiking in the mountains. When you're hiking in the mountains, you experience true fulfillment.

But suppose you live in Kansas, which is almost completely flat ground. How would you respond to that fact?

Strange as it may seem, some people respond simply by being unhappy and complaining about it. They blame Kansas for not having mountains like Colorado. They blame something they feel is keeping them in Kansas—whether it's a job, family ties, or some other responsibility—but they don't make it their first priority to go somewhere where they can experience happiness.

The truth is that many people like that are actually made happy by being unhappy. If that were not the case, why wouldn't they make some meaningful changes?

When you start to identify what makes you happy from the perspective of your soul self, you have to be precise and diligent. You can't just imagine it; you have to visualize it with all your senses.

If hiking in the mountains makes you happy, you have to know which mountains make you happiest. You have to close your eyes and see the trees and flowers that grow in those mountains, especially if they don't grow anywhere else.

Should you also think about how you're going to get to those mountains? Should you worry about the hassle of making a plane reservation or when your boss will let you take time off from work?

No, absolutely not. That's not your concern. The Universe will give you what you want when that desire is an accurate expression of who you are in this present moment, together with a connection to who you are in your authentic, original wholeness.

Once you have an absolutely clear mental picture of what you want and need for happiness, the vehicle will appear. Don't put your attention on the vehicle. Put your attention on what you really want.

Suppose you want to make a telephone call to someone who is really important to you. Just hearing that person's voice will make you extremely happy. Maybe you're far from home in a hotel room, and you really want to make that call.

You look at the cell phone on the nightstand beside the bed in that lonely hotel room. What thoughts go through your mind?

Do you worry about how the phone works, or whether it will work at all? Do you stress about the complex series of neuromuscular processes that must take place in order for you to reach for the phone? What about the possibility that the phone might explode when you touch it?

None of these things concern you because you know that the phone is just a vehicle for fulfilling your intentions, and you have total confidence in that vehicle.

What if you didn't have that confidence? What if you had never seen or used a cell phone before? You might expend so much energy wondering about the phone's inner workings that you never actually make the call.

When you're thinking about what makes you happy, don't immediately think about how you're going to get it. The Universe will provide the transport vehicle—that can mean money—provided you have created a complete, detailed description of your destination.

The vehicle for fulfilling your dream will seem to appear suddenly. I say "seem to" because it's actually been there all along. You just weren't ready to see it and use it. ●

CHAPTER EIGHT

Faster or Slower?

Accelerant: something that speeds up a process.

Deterrent: something that restrains and restricts action.

When you think about vehicles that will take you from where you are now to a life of wealth and happiness, you should realize that some vehicles go faster than others. The speed of your own vehicle depends entirely on you. It depends on whether you choose to step on the gas or step on the brake. Some vehicles go faster than others, and some even go in the wrong direction; you'll need to be prudent and mindful of your chosen vehicle's trajectory.

Thoughts, feelings, or actions that move you quickly in the direction you want to go are called accelerants. Naturally, deterrents do the opposite. There are many accelerants and deterrents in everyone's life, so let's look at a few of them now. These are not necessarily the most important elements in either category, but I hope they'll get you thinking about what slows you down or speeds you up.

My personal favorite accelerant is punctuality. I like to always be on time. It's also an accelerant when those you work with are on time; it shows respect for one another as well as for the project at hand.

On a much larger scale, it shows congruence with the Universe itself—the Universe is always on time. This is what nature intended. If the sun is scheduled to rise at five fifty-three tomorrow morning, you can bet the ranch that it will happen at that exact minute.

When I realized how punctual the Universe is, I decided to duplicate that in my own life. Being consistently on time has definitely been an accelerant in my career. On the other hand, I tend to lose confidence in people who are chronically late, even by just a few minutes.

Tithing is another powerful accelerant, particularly for financial wealth building. Tithing is the ancient philanthropic practice of donating a portion of your income—usually 10 percent—to a worthy charitable cause. Tithing is often associated with religious practices, but it doesn't have to be. Anyone, even atheists, can give away money.

Why is tithing an accelerant for wealth? Doesn't giving away money diminish your net worth? Well, it may do that in terms of raw numbers. But as we've pointed out earlier, there's more to genuine wealth than just dollars and cents, and tithing has a beneficial effect on several of those larger issues.

One of the best things about tithing, especially if your income is currently low, is that tithing makes you feel rich. That's why I encourage everyone to tithe no matter where they are on the financial spectrum. If you act rich, if you see yourself as wealthy in as much detail as possible, you're opening a channel to wealth in the real world.

Both punctuality and tithing can be valuable accelerants, but if I had to choose one action that would do more than anything else to generate wealth, I have no doubt what it would be.

This accelerant is stunningly simple to put into words. However, it takes a bit of effort to put into action, but it's worthwhile. Are you ready? Here is the granddaddy of wealth-building accelerants.

In a word, you must become an *extrovert*. You must meet as many new people as possible. It does not matter who they are. In fact, if you pay too much attention to who you're going to meet, it will slow down the process. It's purely a numbers game, but you must really meet those people. You must exchange names and contact information. That's all there is to it. The more people you meet, the more powerful this accelerant will be. If you meet two new people, that's twice as good as meeting one. If you meet four, that's twice as good as meeting two. If you can fully harness the power of this accelerant, your life will change for the better. Doors will open for you in every area, whether it's financial wealth, a better career, or new relationships. It takes some effort, as very few people are born extroverts.

I didn't know this principle from the beginning, but I saw the power of meeting new people when I had one of my very first jobs. I was a high school dropout (or kick out) with some brushes with the law on my record. I got a job as a bellman at a hotel in Atlantic City. That job gave me a chance to meet a lot of people, and I did my best to make a good impression.

Eventually, I met someone who saw my potential and offered me another job. That would not have happened if I'd been sitting in a room by myself.

What about deterrents to wealth building? We've said that the transformation vehicle will appear when you're ready for it. But you also have to step on the gas and not step on the brakes. You've got to put the key in the ignition to start the car. You can't start the car by letting the air out of the tires. But that's exactly what deterrents cause you to do in your finances and in your life as a whole.

Generally speaking, deterrents take the form of what I call "exclusionary rule setting." You put conditions on what you are willing to do in order to reach a goal. You want to build wealth, for example, but you insist on doing that on your own terms.

The Universe doesn't work that way. The Universe will provide you with opportunities, but those opportunities won't be tailored to your precise expectations. When I was getting started in business, the type of work I was doing was nothing I would ever have expected. But I couldn't say, "This seems unfamiliar, and it makes me uncomfortable, so I'll wait until something just perfect comes along."

When something seems uncomfortable, that's often a defining characteristic of a real opportunity. It's a challenge that can help you grow. It's a big mistake to say, "I don't do windows." Do the windows! Learn to accept the challenge. ●

CHAPTER NINE

Waiting Is the Hardest Part

There are hundreds of books on success and wealth building. Many of these books even understand that real wealth requires more than money. In fact, almost every possible emotion and experience of wealth has been explored and analyzed. But some of the most important elements haven't gotten the attention they deserve. These are the qualities of character that are most needed when you are being tested—and believe me. You will be tested.

If you pass the tests, you will be richer, and, more importantly, you will be wiser. If you don't pass the tests, you will only have yourself to blame. It's as simple as that.

Truthenomics teaches the importance of taking actions, being proactive, and even aggressive, in reaching your goals. But sometimes resilience is just as important; sometimes we have to wait, we have to be patient.

Every day, or even every hour, we face the challenge of waiting for something or waiting for someone: at a traffic light, in a checkout line at the grocery store, waiting for a job interview, or worst yet, waiting in a doctor's office. These are just the annoying but relatively harmless forms of waiting. Other examples are a lot more challenging or even frightening.

Often there are ways to speed up the waiting process, but sometimes there's nothing you can do but wait. Situations like that can be very difficult unless you've developed a capacity for resilience and patience.

With this in mind, I've created a principle that I call "The Seven to Ten Year Rule." The Rule teaches that whenever you open a business, change your career, or embark on any major new endeavor, you will generally need as long as ten years to become a master and for the business to start making your fortune. If you're hyper-motivated, super conscientious, and absolutely relentless in your pursuit, you may be able to accomplish this in as little as seven years. Researchers who have done studies on this subject have arrived at the same numbers.

Most people aren't failures. They just expect things to happen in time frames that are completely unrealistic. So, they're sad forever. That sadness is built on a faulty understanding of the facts. As happens so often, this is a detour from the truth.

Here's the worst byproduct of this detour: people get super fired up about something and try it, but around year four, they think they've come to the end of the line, and they end up quitting. In truth, they were only halfway there; they were on the 50-yard line and gave up any opportunity to reach the end zone. Often, they've already quit a career in which they may have been mildly successful in order to start something new—and now, after investing four or five years in their new career, they quit again. Before they know it, forty years have gone by, and they have changed course ten times in ten different directions, all with the same result.

When you pick the object of your desire from your merged self, and you have a realistic time frame (which I honestly feel is ten years), then you become hugely conscientious—because you know you're on a track that can save a few years if you do things the right way. The right attitude comes from this mix of patience and determination: "It's going to take longer than I thought. It's going to be harder than I thought. On many days I'll feel like I have to give up. But I won't make that decision until I get to the ten-year mark."

But here's the best part of this perspective. Yes, reaching mastery will take longer. Yes, success may be harder to achieve. Likewise, it will pay ten times more, will be ten times bigger, and will bring ten times more joy than you ever imagined. The ten years you invested were like the time required for clearing the land to build a beautiful new house. Then, for the rest of your life, you get to live in it. As you're driving your bulldozer or steamroller in the early years, be aware that this is a wonderful way to go forward.

Something I've noticed recently is how people seem to have lost their stamina. We used to be so strong, and we used to teach our children to be strong. Now, being strong seems like a negative, as if we're not being sensitive enough. In the real world,

I can assure you that's not true. From the medicine—from the Mother—I've learned that she wants us to be grown-up. I see so many people complaining about things that they don't do anything about. They might go to a protest once a year and talk about it for the next 364 days but do nothing. They want an instant result, but they don't understand how results come from a combination of both action and patience.

Patience is a completely internal process. It's inside you rather than outside. You can't weigh patience on a scale, you can't calculate it like a bank statement, and you can't have it in your pocket until you need to take it out. Because it is so subjective, you often can't tell whether someone is patient or impatient just by looking at them. The person next to you in a waiting room may be burning up with impatience, but all you see is a person leafing through a magazine. People looking at you may see a perfectly serene individual. Little do they know how furious you are that the dentist is running late!

Since patience is an internal experience, I want to give you an internal tool for developing it. I want you to grasp the simple fact that your ability to control external events is limited or nonexistent, so you *must* learn to control your inner responses.

You must learn to control your anger, frustration, and anxiety. Fortunately, those responses are *always* within your control, no matter what's happening in the physical world. Just never surrender, never give up!

For thousands of years, this has been the foundation of major spiritual traditions across the world. From India, for example, the Bhagavad Gita advises us, "Be established in timelessness and perform action in the world." This means we should do the best we can in our daily lives, but we should also seek to detach ourselves from the physical outcome, especially in the short term.

Here are some specific suggestions for developing that perspective:

- **Get comfortable with the fact that most things, including wealth building, take time.**

  Often, they take more time than we would prefer. Be prepared for impatience and do your best to embrace those moments and let them go.

- **Reframe your perspective on who you have become over time, who you are in your timeless, authentic self, and what you really want now and in the future.**

  At the same time, don't become preoccupied with what happened yesterday or what might happen tomorrow. Live each new day as a fresh start, filled with limitless possibilities.

- **Instead of trying to do everything at once, break down larger objectives into short-term and medium-term categories.**

  Many people who have difficulty with patience, anger, or frustration—or lots of other things, for that matter—think they're beyond help and can't change. That's a type of reverse arrogance, a deflected way of asserting that you're completely unique. But you're not the most messed up person who ever lived. More difficult people than you have made fundamental changes in their lives, and I may be one of those people.

- **Become aware of the frustrations of other people's lives.**

  Everyone has their own obstacles, crises, setbacks, and relapses. Your plans and needs are not the only things people are thinking about. In fact, your needs shouldn't be the only thing you're thinking about either.

Is it easy to develop patience? The clear and simple answer is "No." Patience is probably one of the most challenging elements of *Truthenomics* to master. Time and energy are required. Patience does not

come easily. That's because, like real wealth itself, it's
not supposed to come too easily. ●

ABOUT THE AUTHOR

Gerard Armond Powell is a leading conscious entrepreneur, thought leader, philanthropist and public speaker whose mission is to transform lives. He is the founder of Rythmia Life Advancement Center in Costa Rica, the "go-to" facility for a spiritually awakening vacation experience. For many years, Gerard was living the "American Dream"—a multi-millionaire who had it all. Deep down, he knew something was missing. The more he achieved, the more he fell into depression. Through a personal crisis, struggling with drugs, alcoholism and thoughts of suicide, he was initiated into a journey of self-transformation. He traveled the world and spent hundreds of thousands of dollars in search of every healing modality he could find. He was inspired to create Rythmia through a powerful encounter with plant medicine that transformed and liberated him from a lifetime of suffering. Gerard now spends his days living at the resort and guides each guest seeking their personal transformation. Over 94 percent of the guests, have reported that they received their "miracle.'" This led Gerard to create this book as a tool to help many others. https://rythmia.com ●